A RED
Poetry
PAINTBOX

CHOSEN BY JOHN FOSTER

OXFORD

UNIVERSITY PRESS

Oxford University Press, Great Clarendon Street, Oxford OX2 6DP

Oxford New York
Athens Auckland Bangkok Bogotá Buenos Aires
Calcutta Cape Town Chennai Dar es Salaam
Delhi Florence Hong Kong Istanbul Karachi
Kuala Lumpur Madrid Melbourne Mexico City
Mumbai Nairobi Paris São Paulo Shanghai
Singapore Taipei Tokyo Toronto Warsaw

and associated companies in
Berlin Ibadan

Oxford is a trade mark of Oxford University Press

First published in paperback 1994
Reissused in this edition 2001

A CIP catalogue record for this book is available
from the British Library

Illustrations by

George Buchanan, Sue Cony, Wendy Crowdy, Karen Donnelly,
Fiona Dunbar, Caroline Ewen, Amanda Hall, Leslie Harker,
Jon Higham, Thelma Lambert, Bill Piggins, Susie Poole,
Amelia Rosato, Sami Sweeten, Susan Winter, Merida Woodford.

ISBN 0 19 919393 2

Printed in Hong Kong

Contents

Mixing colours

Mix red and blue for purple,
Mix red and white for pink,
Mix red and black and yellow
And you'll get brown, I think.

Why don't you mix some colours?
Mix two or three or four.
You might just mix a colour
No-one's ever mixed before.

Eric Finney

I like colours

I like blue.
I like the sky
where birds fly high.

6

I like yellow.
I like the sun
when we have fun.

I like green.
I like frogs
as still as logs.

I like black.
I like the dark
when foxes bark.

Pie Corbett

Traffic lights

Red at the top
Says 'You must stop'.

Red and amber between
Say 'Get ready for green'.

Green below
Says 'You can go'.

John Foster

Golden chips

Brown potatoes, white potatoes,
Change them if you can.
Turn them into golden chips,
Frying in the pan.

Anon

Roses are red

Roses are red,
Spiders are black,
Don't look now
But there's one on your back!

Anon

Animal alphabet

A for an *Ant*,
B for a buzzing *Bee*,
C for the *Cat*,
which climbs up the tree.

D for *DANGER*!
Beware of the *dog*!
E for *Elephant*,
F for *Frog*.

G for *Goat*,
H for *Hare*.
I is for me,
sitting here in this chair!

J for *Jackdaw*,
K for *Kangaroo*,
L for the *Lion*,
which is laughing at you!

M for a *Monkey*,
N for a *Newt*,
O for the *Owl*,
which gives a hoot.

P for a *Panda*,
Q for a *Quail*,
R for the *Rat*,
with its scaly tail.

S for the *Snake*,
which hisses and bites.
T for the *Tiger*,
which snarls and fights.

U for the *Unicorn*,
which lives in fairy tales.
V for *Vulture*,
W for *Whales*.

X in extinct —
Things not living any more,
As dead as the dodo
And the dinosaur.

Y for a *Yak*,
And also for *You!*
Z for the *Zebra*,
The last in our zoo.

John Foster

Alphabet game

I can spell *alphabet*,
as you can see.
How many words
can you make out of me?

John Foster

What is long?

A river flowing to the sea.
A blue whale.

A runway for a jumbo jet.
A dinosaur's tail.

John Foster

25

Large and small

Think of a giant,
Then think of a mouse,
Think of a palace,
Then think of a house,

Think of an eagle,
Then think of a wren,
Think of a wrist watch,
Then think of Big Ben!

Daphne Lister

Elephant and ant

An elephant is so large
that it can stand
outside my window
and blow on my hand.

28

An ant is so small
that it can crawl
through a tiny crack
in the garden wall.

John Foster

29

Jack Hall

Jack Hall,
He is so small,
A mouse could eat him,
Hat and all.

Anon

Giants

A giant is only a giant
To someone very small.
And that's why I'll never be
Afraid of a giant at all!

Irene Yates

The giant and the boy

'I'm tall,' said the giant,
'As tall as a tree.
You're short, little boy,
You can't touch my knee.'

'I'm fat,' said the giant.
He gave a big grin.
'I won't gobble you up.
You're much too thin.'

John Foster

Thin and fat

Thin things:
A piece of cotton,
A bit of string,
A drinking straw,
A pencil,
A pin.

Fat things:
A huge tree trunk,
A hippo's belly,
An air balloon,
A giant jelly.

John Foster

A circle is

A round hoop.
A bowl of soup.

The sun in the sky.
An apple pie.

A cotton reel.
A bicycle wheel.

Pie Corbett

Square, so there!

How many sides has
a big, blue square?
Just four!
How many sides has
a small, red square?
Still four!

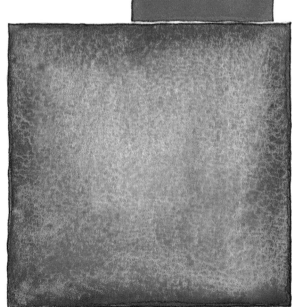

How many sides has
ANY kind of square?
ALWAYS four, so there!

Judith Nicholls

Triangles

There's a triangle I sit on.
It's a triangle I like.
It's there in the middle
of my new, red bike.

There are triangles of paper.
They're green and red and white.
The wind blows them across the sky,
when I fly my kite.

But the best kind of triangles
are the ones I eat,
triangles of chocolate,
my favourite sweet.

Tony Mitton

Moons

The new moon is curved,
like a banana in the sky.

The old moon is round,
like a football kicked up high.

John Foster

Woof

One, two,
How do you do?

Three, four,
Lie on the floor.

Five, six,
I can do tricks.

Seven, eight,
Up at the gate.

Nine, ten,
Let's do it again.

Ian Larmont

Shopping basket

I bought two loaves of bread.
I bought one piece of meat.
I bought three big, green apples.
I bought one sticky sweet.
I bought one custard pie.
How many things did I buy?

Charles Thomson

Zoo dream

I dreamed I went
to the zoo one day.
All the animals
came out to play.
There were

Ten whales whistling,
Nine hippos hopping,
Eight monkeys marching,
Seven lions laughing,

Six snakes skipping,
Five donkeys dancing,
Four crocodiles clapping,

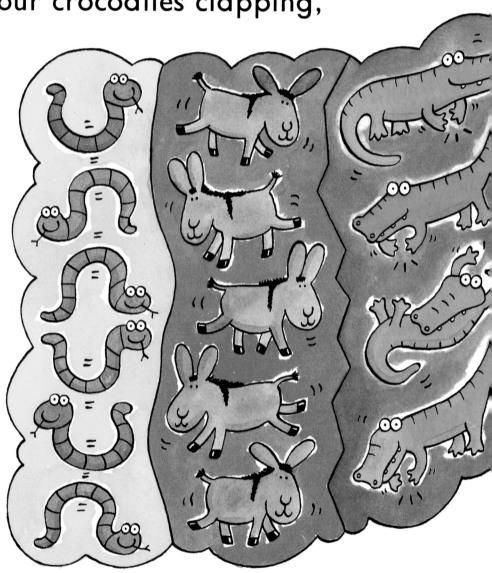

Three rhinos roaring,
Two giraffes giggling
And one seal snoring!

John Foster

In bed again

One, two, three, four!
Lost my temper,
slammed the door.

Five, six, seven, eight!
Licked the gravy
from my plate.

Nine, ten!
In bed again!

John Foster

That's hot

Flames from a dragon.
Water boiling in a pot.

A blazing fire.
The desert sun.
That's hot!

John Foster

Summer and winter

In winter,
It is so cold
That the water in the lake
Freezes into a thick slice
Of ice.

In summer,
It is so hot
That I take my shirt off
And jump in the pool
To get cool.

John Foster

Keeping warm

I wish I had
Thick white hair,
Like a polar bear,
To keep me warm
When the cold wind blows
And it snows.

But my skin is thin,
So I have a thick coat
To wrap myself in,
To keep me warm
When the cold wind blows
And it snows.

John Foster

The snowman says

I like it when it's cold,
When the north wind blows,
When it snows and it freezes
My nose and my toes.

I don't like it when it's hot,
When it's sunny all day,
When my nose is runny
And I melt away.

John Foster

On cold winter nights

On cold winter nights
it freezes and snows,
and my hot water bottle
toasts my toes.

John Foster

Index of first lines

Acknowledgements

The Editor and Publisher are grateful for permission to include the following poems:

Pie Corbett for 'A circle is' and 'I like colours' both © 1994 Pie Corbett; Eric Finney for 'Mixing colours' © 1994 Eric Finney; John Foster for 'Animal alphabet', 'Alphabet game', 'Elephant and ant', 'The giant and the boy', 'Thin and fat', 'What is long?', 'That's hot', 'Summer and winter', 'The snowman says', 'Keeping warm', 'On cold winter nights', 'Traffic lights', 'Zoo dream' and 'In bed again' all © 1994 John Foster; Ian Larmont for 'Woof' © 1994 Ian Larmont; Tony Mitton for 'Triangles' © 1994 Tony Mitton; Judith Nicholls for 'Square, so there!' © 1994 Judith Nicholls; Charles Thomson for 'Shopping basket' © 1994 Charles Thomson; Irene Yates for 'Giants' © 1994 Irene Yates.